# COLOUR THEORY

Worcester's Student
Poetry Society and friends

Colour Theory



Cover design and illustrations by Freddie Barker

Published by Mini Poetry Press 2023
www.minipoetrypress.com

ISBN: 978-1-916838-00-0

# COLOUR THEORY

## Contents

# Foreword

In a high-speed world of vast monotony, literature and the creative arts provide pockets of spectral insight and kaleidoscopic magic. This book is dedicated to:

The fiery go-getters; hot-headed drivers; full-hearted, cherry-picked curators; passion-driven divas; blush-cheeked lovers; the enraged; the tenacious; the relentless forces to be reckoned with, and those with a pair of crimson horns protruding from their heads.

The playful conversationalists; enthused innovators with a citrus charm; the whimsical; the imaginative; the warm. The inspired; the never-tired masterminds; the monarch butterflies with regal wings; the breeze-blown autumn leaves, and those pouring with zest.

The good-as-gold; old souls; forever young adventurers; the enlightened; the excited, the charitable chalices brimming with hope. Those who seek success, those with more ideas than time to realise them; those who feel revitalised spring's daffodils. The radiant, aloof, and loyal friends who ooze with soothing melodies.

The ever-growing achievers, the green-thumbed, the envious, the trivial, the ambiguous. Those grounded by their own roots; those who learn by second nature; the down-to-earth mediators; the wallflowers who cower behind ivy; the unruly and mischievous.

The turbulent and storm-swept, the emotional, the compassionate, the calmly simmering in a bubble bath; the anxious, and the wise. Those with eyes like summer skies, the forgetful, the regretful, the silent readers, the day-dreamers, those in recovery; those yet to find their niche; and those learning to venture into the unknown.

Your vibrance - chromatic and unfiltered - powers the unseen world around us. Because you, reading this, are part of the magic.

BERRIES

## Pomegranate

By Freddie Barker

from bud to bloom.
seed to fruit.
ripened by the sun.

pick me, take
each loose pip as a
token of my desire.

pick apart my pomegranate heart -
rip into the toughened flesh;
harsh crimson stains your fingertips
you bite and scorn the binding threads.

tear apart my words, my love,
beating, bleeding - my life's longing - fleeting.
a lamb to the slaughter, i dye your lips as you're eating.
a thousand little pieces of punctured life leaving
burst between your teeth
bittersweet and seething.

you overindulge.
you're not satisfied.
i'm seedless. an empty shell.
no longer crisp and fresh, just sore –
a fragile mesh, a mess, undressed.
i hurt but you crave more.

## Pass Port

By Damon Lord

Sweet, strong, the rich ruby wine
moves down the table, hand to fellow hand
Raise a glass to friendship!

disaster
        spill
        falls
                splashes
        liquid liberty leaks, runs, spreads…
                And is blocked.

the steward's obsidian cloth (supposedly beautiful blue)
declares triumph; with mirth, imposes new additional rules
Freedom of movement halted.
Hands no more joined together.

## Toby Jug

By D.D. Holland

Just hollow.

If words are glued together by feelings

Then mine are a snapped string of pearls

Skitting across the floor

Tripping me up.

I slip slide towards what I'm trying to say,

Then miss it, by a hazel hairsbreadth.

Maybe if I didn't shiver and stutter

And sleep too much or not at all

I would stand a better chance.

But as it is,

I am a wordsmith who can't speak,

Can't write,

Can't feel,

Just hollow.

## Wear Rouge Or Pink

By Carriad Morgana

My mother's generation said that I should paint rouge or pink
onto my skin to make the boys wink,
I think.

My dad said I should stay home, read a book,
don't give those boys another look,
to catch you like a fish on a hook.

Decades later, I realise that I'd followed mum's advice for years,
not knowing that it would ultimately end in tears,
Dad understood that men simply charm away your fears.

Because he was a man and know that men flatter you with words so sweet,
when you're young and innocent and menstruating heat.
Their only aim is for you naked on top of a sheet.

Until you ultimately realise that they say you have lovely eyes
to only get in-between your juicy pink moist thighs.
When you finally become aware, it's them you despise.

Don't paint yourself in pink to make the boys wink.
Wear whatever the hell you think
suits you. Some men stink!!

## Poppy

By Susan Wood

Your blush is of blood,

Initial flush, emerging

Womanhood. First show

Of frilled, carmine, sanguine red-

Your seasoned coming of age.

## Lagoon Pockets

By Rhianna Levi

Bruising eczema lines my pockets,
The dips of my hips and the permanent indent of my pinky finger.
Coming and going as a mistake,
Rewinding in an ASMR playlist- without lagoon peace
and instead a dotty iron deficiency.
Burning off energy pours and pounds and parks in clashing ways,
I'll display my plum blemishes whilst I play.

## I Scrape Seeds From A Pomegranate

By L. E. Wynn

and the juice washes my eyes purple as vineyard grapes,
makes my vision cloudy like that of wine-drunk women,
settles on my corneas as joy.

I discover that pomegranate dyes fabric
when a stray droplet stains my blouse.
I imagine crushing each seed
into a large wooden barrel,
winemaker-style, and cast
all my whites, off-whites
and creams into it,
soaking them in summer.

I daydream about draping them
on sun-heated rocks, popping
grapes in my mouth and smile at
how the juice settles in the wrinkles
of my lips like the dye does
in the creases of the linen.
When dried, they will clothe me royal.

## A Harrowing

By Ellie Dart

The phoneline is empty again,

I'm hunting for vibrations in the mixed

signals. Omens from the ghosts.

In horror lexicon – choose

left. or right.

bring your colour to their circuit,

in pink/red – a lover's warning?

I attest.

## The Scarlet Woman

By Chaz Jubin

A stain upon my collar,
Tarnishing my body,
Covering my flesh in a vermillion hue.
I'll try and abolish any reminder of this blemish,
A record I'll carry wherever I travel,
They'll stop and Stare, ponder:
'Is that the Scarlet Woman?'
They'll never begin to wonder,
Did I deserve the perdition?
Sentenced without judge and jury.
A glance at the reflection of an unfamiliar body,
It stares back with tear wrecked eyes,
Clumps of black cascading,
With every blink, every movement.
Silently screaming:
'Do you remember before?'
'Only when I'm dreaming'
My head hangs heavy
With burdens thrust upon me,
Sleep is an escape
But for an expensive fee.
The World stopped at that exact moment,
When my being forever changed,
Stripped of my dignity, life, and comfort
A lost soul begging for a home
Cast out to the side
'You're spitting lies'
They'll proclaim
As they gnaw at my carcass
And dig claws into my bones
Just another wasted child
Thrown into a cardinal pile.

## Pink (Not As In The Colour But As In The Pains)

By Amelie Simon

I love the word pink in a way I do not love the colour.
The cavern of my throat takes the word pink and makes it mean
lonely, cold, and hazardous. It takes the word pink
and filters it through stalactite teeth,
shows that it actually means wounds and
that feels more right than the sky, or the painters,
who take pink and make it mean cradles and lovers.
I pull a plum apart and let it blot my palms,
bloom into a growing pool of losses that will be
but are just fructose stains for now. I do not eat it.
I take the word pink and scrub the pastels from it,
treat it like how a mechanic treats rust,
treat it like how I treat blood clots in the shower's plug.
I take the word pink and make it a blade, wield it like one.
It is the colour of mouths and bruised palms,
of the water I wring from the cloth into the sink.
The apple blossom must understand how it is to hurt,
surely that is how it knows to be pink.

## I Left Mr Rochester

By D.D. Holland

I could have stayed with him that day.
Legs knotted around his waist,
Nose buried in his hair,
And conceded.
I could have admitted that I didn't really care
about the woman in the attic.
That madness was a by-product of loving him.

I felt no holy glow, or godly wrath,
Just the rattle of my mother's rune-carved bones,
The raven feathers on my great-grandmother's back
Rustling as she wailed:
A lie is the necrosis of respect
Take the hammer to your heart
Before he takes it to your head

His wandering hand was tender as bruised meat,
the bloodied knuckles of his striking fist, silken
Oh, too quick would I have let his silver tongue
Lick its way back up my thigh and into my heart.

## Selfless Fervour

By Jay Rose Ana

In an enchanted forest, not far from here.
Where passions dwell, a humble berry patch flourished.
Amidst verdant emerald leaves, ruby-red berries shine;
— like tiny hearts bursting with selfless fervour.

A young maiden, seeking her heart's desire,
ambled one summer upon this brightly lit patch.
Intrigued, she tasted a ruby-red berry,
a surge of emotions overcame her;
— a kaleidoscope of flavours, sweet, tangy, and intense.

Each berry whispered love's secrets, igniting her soul.
Their tender tales of passion, once a symphony untold.
She tended her dreams, nurturing her newfound passion.
In fertile soil of hope, she flourished with compassion.

As her love for berries grew, so did her love for life.
In this tiny ruby-red berry patch, her summer was bright.
She found new courage to unlock depths of her heart.
Through berry's embrace, her love's journey did impart.

That forest lives on, not far from here.
That red-berry patch, though overgrown,
Lays in wait for new heart's desire.
And new dreams to be sown.

## Opposites Attract

By Eleni Brooks

we are a mess of tangled

limbs, an awkward intertwining of

mismatched jigsaw pieces

mouth to mouth

(not in the way you're thinking)

making our bed in everyday

moments, I

am privileged to sink

deep into your shuddering resentment

to touch, your heart bounds

*I love you* on repeat

until doubts drown

& breathes synch &

*I'm found* echoes each beat

## A Classic Red Lip

By Bryoney Cook

Small eyes watch her mother,
painting her face with ritual care.
A meditation in beauty, each brushstroke
enhancing the blank canvas curves of her features.

But she is already beautiful.
Though young, she understands
the need to look your best, but who decided
this had to be under layers of paint?
Strip everything back - what is left?

She is beautiful. Kind.
A cloud of heavy scent fills the room.
Poison, by the mirror,
as her mother paints her cheeks,
rouge leaving behind a wash of colour.

She is beautiful. Kind. Loving.
Watching in awe as a transformation
takes place in front of her,
eyelids expertly coloured for the occasion
and mascara defines the laughter lines.

She is beautiful. Kind. Loving. Funny.
Her mother pouts, pencil lines drawn.
A brush picks up the ruby red
a tissue blots.
A Rorschach created by lipstick.

She is beautiful. Kind. Loving. Funny. Colourful.
She tells her mother she looks pretty.

No, that she always looks pretty.
Mother hugs her tightly with one arm and her eyes water.
"And you always smell nice" raises a laugh.
She is unaware.

She is beautiful. Kind. Loving. Funny. Colourful.
She stands at the mirror, all grown.
Painting her own face in the same ritual.
The self-doubt they share, yet was never shared.
Those small eyes stare back at her.
You are beautiful. Kind. Loving. Funny. Colourful.
You are your mother's daughter.

## Rose Colored Glasses

By Tommy Bjørheim

His toxic fumes smell like a floral perfume

His daggers that pierce my skin are a warm embrace

His sharp, deadly claws gently caress my cheek, wiping away the tears

His yellow teeth that regularly rip the flesh from my bones feel like kisses on my skin

His roars of hatred are sweet nothings he whispers in my ear

His internal monster is covered up by a cuddly teddy bear

The constant combat between us is a slow dance on the pink clouds

His punches feel like a fairytale, and the kicks like magic

His aggressive rejections are the apologies from my father, I never received

His awfulness is my perfection

Because when I look at him through rose colored glasses, the red flags

Just look like

Flags.

## Blush

By Sage White-Drake

The rush of blood.
The coursing red flood.

It settles on your cheeks, your face.
It tingles with warmth and heat.
You feel odd, out of place.
You want to melt into the street.

Could it be?
Dare I dream?
Was that smile returned to me?
My anxiety brain screams!

Welcome to flirting done badly.
Where discomfort rules the mind.

You never think it'll be acknowledged.
You're used to being left behind.

For now though, biology rules, its taken hold.
You're grinning like a maniac and looking a bit full on.

Let's enjoy the feeling, for good or bad.

Let's see what comes from this.

Use the warmth, feel the glow.

After all, if you never try, you'll surely never know.

## Bedroom Warfare

By Rhi Armstrong

Our bedroom became a war ground.
We dug trenches with pillows and
buried our dead bodies beneath the blankets.
Disputing the barricades made
of backs turned on one another
when the conversation become too coarse for soft flesh.
And while it is for our own protection,
the space between us can't help but
feel like an abyss of infinite uncertainty.
You counted your rounds,
I licked my wounds free of infection.
You clock a gun into my head,
and I am forced to turn around
and face it.
Face you.
Destruction looms at the edges
as we tossed and turned on the sheets
like battleships upon waves,
crashing against one another.
We are dying like a sinking ship
and while you're content to just let it,
I try to steer us to safety and
salvage pieces of two broken hearts
until all that's left are memories of what once was.
The slow decay of flesh and bone and secrets.
We play at war,
night after night, fight after fight.
And tomorrow?
Distance will swallow us for breakfast.

## Bruises

By Niamh Baxter

The bruise that hugs my hip transports me to another time,
of climbing trees,
sword fights using broken branches,
jumping into rivers,
into the vegetable patch,
to grab the caterpillar cutting holes into the cauliflowers.
Gentle skin mottled with stories,
each purple stain a new tale,
the graze on my knee forms a new narrative,
the cut on my palm, each scarlet bead holds history,
scabs from the trip to the zoo,
a scar that utters words about falling off bikes,
black eyes from flying tennis balls,
a loose tooth from a game of tag,
the perfect imperfections that tell stories.
Blink,
and I'm back,
staring down at the bruise that hugs my hip.
Grin,
staring down at another story added to the pages of my skin.

## A Wound Like A Summer Night

By Zoe Dempsey Martínez

There's a tear in the middle of my room.
Its frayed edges splinter under sunlight like incense smoke
and when you run your fingers through, they catch
in threads of tendon, wisps of bedsheets and wasp wings.

The tear is the deep bruise red of a girl you kiss with your eyes open,
a girl like a skipping stone, a night like a lake.
An old bed like a dock, its creaking bows tangled in lotus and cattail.
A garnet sky bleeds the lakeside of my room black,
the back woods climb us with bird cry and cicada thrum.

There's a tear in the middle of my chest.
Mouth of wolf, dead dove breast, hunting ground, tire tracks.
Red like love these days, cherries dying gorgeously between your teeth,
the violence of melancholy ruining tablecloth like spilled wine.

When you run your fingers through it, I splinter.
My skin of hammock string, stirred tides and locust wing,
I bleed out a night sky.

## The House Of Resolution

By Brian Comber

at the appointed hour the doorbell rings,
we have routines and I make drinks
while they try my jigsaw then throw down the pieces,
the incidents of their life lie littered about my house,
I place their washing in the machine and note how long we've got,
we discuss their supervisor who won't let up

as I trail them downstairs,
I listen to their circular argument about opportunity
and comment on their dress code,
they hand me their 'phone when there's no more to say,
I nod, we nod, I pass their clothes into my tumble drier and
in a twenty minute cycle they say they'll leave him,

next time and we discuss the relative merits
of tablet A and tablet B until the spin winds down,
I fold their seven red work shirts
over my arm, an identity for each working day;
they stack their cup. How did I come to be here
watching them as they wind along the path to their car,

to throw their crumpled shirts in the back,
wave once and think about waving twice?
I burst through the spare room into the smoking shelter
with gleaming air con vents and an authentic bully,
I reason with her for two cigarettes
before withdrawing victorious

coated in sweat, while the window frames still rattle,
and their manager remains in the hall
what possessed you to choose red?
I hear myself shout, the danger warning,
the fecundity, the blood;
their partner is pinned to my lawn and I describe

borders, boundaries, limits, and margins, until the birds stop singing.
I rise late at night to descend to the cellar
to argue with Euclidean certainty
that they should be promoted,
weigh up their lost arguments on my kitchen scales,
until the head of HR agrees and fades like a skylark ascending,

in the porch, held for months, a single sob surfaced;
they'll return with fresh wounds to bind, their reds uniformly bleached,
I see them about town, the mysteries of their quotidian world,
the other spaces they inhabit, a red smear skipping down a passage,
merging into crowds at the edge of my vision, exsanguinating,
their thin red threads unravelling.

## Cut My Eyes Open

By Cameron Simpson

Cut my eyes open

Now I see my face

In glorious dark crimson

Colour corrected

Dried and cracked

Eyes on stalks

Second person

A fleshy periscope

A finger in my retina

A new perspective

Through the reds of my eyes

Now I see my face

Cut my eyes open

## After I Awoke As A Vampire (Notes From My Menstrual Cycle, First Draft)

By Kashala Abrahams

It drools with droplets of
blood in its cycle:

Monthly massacre makes
victims vex.

Vampiric visions of
Christ's sin:

His limbs high to the sky of my
crucifix.

Hemoglobin salivates, fizzes, and bulbs every 28 to 35 days.
with
Clots and tears from the eye down

there. ({})

Anaemic each time the vagina eclipses.

## For My Sins

By Rachy xox

Hot breath on my neck, sends my spine to shiver,
Lips press fiercely, and hands that follow.
I'm at your mercy, blissed and free
In this moment it's you versus me.
My skin alive to the you that's upon thee

Movement is quick with purpose and embraced with arms longing,

In this moment it's you versus me.

The night skies moon shines around the space we occupy
Clear as though morning glows, we please the senses
In this moment it's me versus you
Passion roars and breathless I see you
Mighty and placating our bodies entwine
Time stands still and emotions soar
In this moment it's just us
A twin flame in body and soul
Each movement wanted, a story to behold
No questions asked, no questions answered
It's pure and simple, true to its core
For you and me I simply adore

xox

## Hair Dye

By Cat Whitehouse

Picture the scene.
Summer 2020.
The pandemic has the world in a tight grip of fear and panic.
Everyone is buying essentials leaving the shelves bare: flour, toilet roll, hand gel…
Hair dye.

A new colour.
A new identity.
It seems like everyone, and their dog are making 'radical' appearance changes during these crazy
covid times!
But this one is mine.

Purple.
An intense shade of vivid violet.
It's new and exciting.

My partner's gloved hands covered in the magic mixture.
that will turn my faded red into a deep, ravishing rhubarb.
He then swiftly scrubs the excess off my skin before we stop.
And watch.
And wait...

A second attempt is needed for it to really stick,
the red is more resistant than anticipated.
It gives him an additional opportunity to hone his craft.
and learn this vital skill that will dominant his life from this day forward.

It stains the towel as well as my heart.

MAGMA

## The Departure Board

By Lauren Frankland

I always arrive at the train station early
To look at the departure board
Platforms 1 and 2 are going in different directions
And I imagine which journey I could afford,
If I could step on a train and go somewhere new
I guarantee you I'd leave
Because the soft orange glow of the words on the screen
They provide with me a sense of relief
An escape from the daily do-this and do-that
To find somewhere new to explore,
And sometimes I wish that those words would just switch
To not tell me the destination at all
What if I just didn't get on the right train?
And chased the unknown one instead?
Platform 1 train to nowhere calling at blank
A mystery so appealing,

Don't you think?

## Spain 1501, Vibrant Orange

Laura Liptrot

Across my journey, all that I have seen,

Here at Alhambra, in Granada, Spain;

The palace of the Catholic king and queen;

Whose shadows (long) and voices: live again.

Blood oranges: bitter sweet; ripe and round;

Pomegranates and Christ's resurrection;

Castanets, the snapping (wooden) teeth sound;

Waters blazing with the sun's reflection:

Remind me that this is the land of God,

Where angels of the Inquisition reign;

And here, amid the olive trees, have trod –

And manifest here, in the realm of Spain –

The almighty, in ragged human guise,

Holding us firm, in His immortal eyes.

## Crystal Grave

By Ashley Whitehouse

The sky clear as crystal

The glowing blood orange sphere expelling a blast of tremendous heat

The rays of the sun engulf the tear in the fabric of man

As I walk briskly through the garden of death drops of darkness drip down

my sullen face

I trace my fingers across the title of the passed

Shivering, crying, bleeding

As I stood looking at the cold, chilling grave the gusts of wind were amplified

bringing howling voices of lost souls which were once with us.

## Tangerine Sky

By L. E. Wynn

I wonder how many thousands of miles apart
the sunset clouds are. They look as close
as oranges in a fruit bowl, dazzle the sky
with their Citrine glow.

Does the distance between them feel like
our hands when we hold each other,
separated by atoms, the illusion of touching
enough for us to forget trivial things like physics?
Is it as tangible as the taste of tangerine on your tongue
when the word leaves your lips, mouth dry
for a drop of citrus juice?

Or is it the world's last functional lighthouse
on an abandoned island looking
for another to beam its light to
not knowing the rest are dead?

## Autumn Cascade

By Natalie Carr

Along this Autumn trail,
I see a dog's tail,
Wagging with happiness and freedom
As crisp leaves cascade from preserving trees,
Dancing wildly as they fall, waltzing with the breeze.
The reds, oranges, and yellows like a fire ablaze,
Replace the luscious greens before, adorned by summer's haze.
The dog sniffs through Autumn's debris,
Finding hidden treasures obscured from wanderers.
A stick to their delight leads the way,
To an afternoon of endless play.
As a coldness tiptoes like a quiet mouse
Through the fields, down the streams and nipping at your nose,
You feel its bite, the sensation delights,
Autumn has you in its throws.
But how can you feel the sting of ice with such warmth in abundance,
As fire rains from the heaven, leaving beds of comfort,
For small animals to nest within, to hide from hungry stalkers,
For children to kick about in, for sticks to be found by dog walkers,
The temperature may be faltering and falling from good grace,
But there's nothing more beautiful than the colours of Autumn's face.

## Contemplations In Tangerine

By Damon Lord

Sticky, bright orange, paper squares
Decorate textbook layers
Peeking out from deckled edges, filling.
Scribbled jottings caked upon ivory pages,
A platter of my fractured fleeting thoughts,
Fragrant folios build perception's recipe.
Cook cursive communiqués into coherent concepts.
The note block thins, the book thickens,
With mandarin memos flavouring the word and ink tiramisu
Adorning the author's musings with my own.

## The Drive

By Rachy xox

I write this sat alone, I cooked for no one but me
Eating a plateful of boneless ribs and noodles ….
Realising I'm swallowing not battling, enjoying not confined
Feeling happy to feed my body, nourish my soul-
Not skipping another meal for the taste of distain.
Healing to me ….it's standing still, jaw unclenched and arms

relaxed

It's hearing the universe speak my name
Sending messages from wall to wall.

Healing to me is deciding what's a yes and all that's a no
Its feeling free within because, well…. I say it's so.
Adventurous days and silent nights beneath the skies.
Healing to me is not asking permission,
Not shrinking back or hiding on the inside
It's feeling like I was meant to, and enjoying the ride

Healing for me is standing with pride
Knowing my journeys far from over
But with tunes blasting loud
I get to drive

xox

## Crystal Eyes

By Jay Rose Ana

In childhood's depths,

    like magma's hidden might.

A world of wonders,

    yet to witness dreams light.

Innocence flows,

    from a molten core within.

Dreams crystallise,

    young possibilities begin.

In youth's eruption,

    passions overflow.

Like magma surging,

    seeking paths to go.

From depths profound,

    bursting through each day.

With fiery zeal,

    they forge their way.

## Segments

By Ruth Stacey

What we know
is an orange,
segmented, the
fruit, sharp on
our tongues.
There is always
an equal number
of segments.
Black, white
yes, no, open,
closed. Orange.
The peel represents
an unravelling.
Life, this life, is
suffering, so the
monks sing
in their endless
spinning prayers.
Please, pray for
me like George
Harrison prayed.
Endless notes.

## Warm Marmalade

By Chaz Jubin

The day begins,
Warm marmalade on toast,
An ever-present volcanically hot coffee,
A view of the flourishing garden
Covered in hedgehogs and a field of rainbows.
A breeze that rattles the little glass door,
Pouring in smells of a rainstorm just gone.
Sun cascades over her pearly white hair,
Kissing each line etched from wisdom.
Triple strength mints burning cold,
Prompting notions of nostalgia.
Hidden treasure of gold and red wrappers,
Delectable wafers that bless the mind
With moments of peace.
Her stories hold tight to the family who listens,
Each word soothing their soul,
Bodies aching from laughter and joy,
And a familial tie that will last forever,
Listening to Robins sing and remembering.

The day ends,
A soul that's never forgotten,
Lives touched and moulded by her,
She graces each memory like musical beauty,
The world in mourning for an eclectic individual.

## People Who Turned Up After My Ovary Was Removed

By Ash Bainbridge

the friend's boyfriend who gifted a Dairy Milk bar the size of a Yamaha keyboard after driving straight from Cadbury World | the relative who talked so much I pretended to fall asleep | the friend who complained about her period pains too | the floor manager who sent up a balloon as I soaked off iodine in the bath | the family friend who played medic to gain ward access | the girl I was not dating who shipped a card and marigolds | the ex who brought round "Risk" and did not let me win | the friends who posted a box of missed lecture notes 205 miles Second Class | the relative who said she'd known all along | the dog who tried to lick my dressing until the scabs shed |

## Traffic Cones - Day

By Freddie Barker

A
denim-blue
Lexus; its steel
Frame intersects a
Nissan Sentra, pulled
off-centre, skewed on the

side-line of the A5. A delicate
wreck; the plateaued signature
of a spiderweb splinters across the
windscreen. Radial hazard beams light the
stage of a collision unforeseen, and beyond the
layers of hungover turbulence, a parade of traffic

cones line the scene. The biting wind nips and tucks the
folds that nest within the crest of a once-streamlined bumper,
now crumpled like paper, crunched upon impact. The molten tarmac
soaks up oil, littered with ash and strewn shards of glass, tatters of air bags
that burst at the seams; and an air-freshener hangs meekly beneath a
disfigured rear-view mirror. And surrounding the charred wreckage,
standing still in the breeze, forefronting stunted remanence
of automobiles, a parade of traffic cones line the scene.

## Traffic Cones - Night

By Freddie Barker

A
valiant
conquest; a
pursuit forged
in the heat of a
moment, spurred

by spirited intuition,
and a glut of jäger bombs
dropped down the throats of
new generation academics, who,
determined and enthralled, began
a voyage: carefully spawned between

drunken sprawls down the street in high-heeled
boots on blistered feet. Will these students risk it all?
The peril of arrest - or a clumsy downfall? Injury– or death
or worse yet – alcohol poisoning on a Wednesday after losing a bet?
Of course not! -- There are no obstacles this brigade can't evade in
exchange for this superior drunken freshers' rampage! So off they go on
their noble quest: an overplayed escapade that dares to compress wisdom,
stamina, liberation and strength; Into a sickly-sweet victory, only felt upon
waking to the sight of a stolen traffic cone.

## Nuclear Hometown

By Cameron Simpson

Somewhere on the Clyde, in a bunker, are the bombs

Hidden, out of sight and out of mind

Through the glow of daybreak, the people sleep away

But as the Cold Wars turn...

The lonely aeroplane drops its burden through the dawn

A soda-can pre-emptive counterstrike

The pale-white morning sun is swallowed by the cloud

Of oranges and greys

The sleeping threat disintegrates as the fire reaches home

There won't be any time to see it come-

A quarter-second blazing from the second sun

Better you than me?

## Marmots

By Ash Cascavilla

High in the mountains,
The sun rises above the peaks
Life returning to the world for another day.
Marmots sneak out of their homes,
Squeaks of joy serenading the world with their excitement.
They are propelled forward by curiosity,
their brown pelts keeping them warm and safe,
but not entirely.
Many seek their blood and meat,
Some flying in the skies,
others slithering on the ground.

The marmots keep a watchful eye for these dangers
Keeping in packs to protect one another
As danger lies in wait.

Humanities modernity has done them no favours in this.
Roads wind and turn in their territory
Limiting them and separating them from one another
Engines roar, sending them into hiding
Cutting their adventures short.

## Clementines

By Zoe Dempsey Martínez

In a house where nobody apologises,
forgiveness tastes like orange peels.

A waxy waning tug that marries my fingertips, tangy white bite
on the tip of my tongue, and a bright pregnant orange, ripe
and resting, nesting the skin of her swollen planet,
tenderly torn, marooned on the counter, cocooned
in a blue kitchen cloth.

I've learnt to use a knife to pry off the coat of light,
but my mother peels suns with her hands.

Her thumbs press open clementines,
henna hair and hazel Kohl eyes
elsewhere, flicking at flies in the Spanish heat,
neat rivulets of honeydew skin dropping into
her lap, bleeding sweetness down her arms
like Sauternes. I wake from a nap drunk on that noble rot,
the room swelling with oranges,

clemens, clinare, clementia, chests cleft left closed again,

wondering when we first died and how many clementines
my mother has peeled since then.

## Do I Not Like Orange?

By Jenny Hope

So-called colour of optimism, of pumpkin-bloody-spice that rears its head
on the first strike of late-summer before kids get their last-minute late-uniform
run of over-priced-out-of-stock shoes and their lethargic demeanours back into school –
of sun and fakened tans that glow Donald and of yielding rubber cheese and faux juice
so full of numbered Es that once ingested give an inner Day-Glo hue – though not
as intense as the radio-active Ready-Brek kid that walked to school in kick-arse-flared jeans
and a mandatory self-exclusion zone – how bitterly disappointed we were to find that despite
parental promises – once ingested this sweetened gruel did no such flaming thing –
the closest we ever saw were strange-tan-tights that your Nan wore for Sunday Best
with a clash of blue-rinse-set-and-finish and a serving of Sunday lunch carrots
because you never see a rabbit in glasses – carrots in their glorified falseness of colour
naturally mutated from when purple was not-quite-right and nothing
to do with The House of flaming Orange and why now orange as a colour
cannot simply not be trusted.

## Pineapple On Pizza

By Niamh Baxter

Tell me a secret,
when we are hidden underneath the blanketed sunset,
the warmth wraps and weaves around us.

Tell me your sorrows,
of the days; today, yesterday, and the tomorrows,
as I watch the sky become a painted masterpiece,
sunshine burns, melts away your wax-coated frown,
as you tell me that we are different,
you and I,

I am the buttercup scattered ground,
and you are the peach tinted sky,
my gilded hello's
and your crimson stained goodbyes,

I try to grab the stars,
you scowl at the birds that fly,
yet your heart wanders,
and mine just lies,
with the grin of my teeth,
with your soft tender sigh,
and your ocean-coloured gaze,
the flecks of yellow in my eye,
sour and sweet,
yet we still try,
take my hand in this moment,
a delicate mixture of two whole worlds made into one,
a circle of concoctions, combinations combined,
the sharp bite of your tongue,
that mellows each time I speak,
how your hand grounds me, stops me from being taken by the breeze,

my dry humour,
grains of sand that fill a desert,
and your guttural, deep laughs that lap over me like waves,
the salt of your tears tastes sweet on my tongue,
as we watch the sky darken,
to a brilliant bronze,
framed in this moment,
differences aside,
because your savoury smirk compliments my sweet smile,
and your cold hand fits perfectly against my warm palm,
like a completed jigsaw.

## Undignified

By Eleni Brooks

sometimes you want to die &

then you dance undignified

in the same day, same place

bowing to fear while you stare it in the face

saying, *you aren't welcome here*

*but life is*

maybe it's the peach schnapps & the pizza

or the two boys on the sofa

but suddenly this morning is

a memory

worth living through

CUSTARD
6
5
4
3
2
1

## Repotted

By Zoe Dempsey Martínez

love and lemons

down my throat

tear my tummy up

plant a lemon seed

in my chest

I'll grow a buttercup

## Life's Architect

By Natalie Carr

Plastic yellow faced figures,
We mould them to our will,
We build our Lego houses,
On a buildable Lego hill.
Each one can be whatever we want,
Their accessory becomes their profession,
And to play with Lego, even as an adult,
Is no longer an embarrassing confession.
For these little plastic people,
With their little plastic lives,
Help us to build the future we want,
The dream that always survives.
And the nostalgia that we feel,
When putting bricks together,
Can keep us occupied inside,
Despite the stormy weather.
And although they have started to recognise,
We all have different coloured skin,
The OG yellow Lego face,
Is where our collections usually begin.
For locked up in this moment,
We are children once more,
Getting inspiration to create
Sitting cross legged on the floor.
And if we build something we're not happy with,
If we want to self-improve,
If there are elements that no longer have relevance,
We can simply just remove.
We are the architects of this world,
The fairy god mother of the story
And every scenario that comes to pass,
Is created by me and for me.

## Stings Of Lemon

By Rhianna Levi

Yellow jackets flood the flower head. Brighter than butter but deathly, merciless, cutting thread- no repairs. Taking in scenery of Northern America in agile steps

Blunt and
Respectable and
Lemon in zest.

## ChoirKid

By Ash Bainbridge

On Sundays,
dawnshine with ingot weight
smashes
    factory
        church
            glass
and casts the coarse collars gold.
Stone-muscle walls bulk mass
with frankincense and myrrh –
    centuries
    stacked –
        veiling B&H
        smoked half-cut
        with flicks out
        the leadlight window.

When sermons drag,
I place one jelly shag band
between my thighs and
jerk the soprano cassock taut,
    shooting the fluorescent loop heavenward.
Prayers are treasured as
elders in gilt pleather
sandals compete for the loudest, "Amen!"
    (Because God only opens The Pearly Gates
    for organs with the w i d e s t pipes.)
My payment is aged rice
paper and port before
chipping sun-bleached pillar wax
after one hot honey
flame-drop
falls.

## Haiku On Yellow

By Susan Wood

PRIMROSES

Primroses spread skirts
of satin: silken tutus
for ballet dancers.

DYING OF LIGHT

Across the Dead Sea
light is dying- rekindling
life and Hope beyond.

LIMONCELLO

Harvested from heat,
Sicilian lemons- a
zesty, sunshine drink.

BUMBLE BEE

That bumble bee, fat
jocund, busy in the joy
of pollination.

DANDELION

Dandelion- bright,
fallen sun, stretched ablaze with
golden pollened rays.

## Dancer In The Sunshine

By Hayden Robinson

I remember

Under the sun bright as a dream,
you flip back from the grass,
a cartwheel show in our garden!

Your muscles, trained and toned, clench,
the tips of your toes point like spears,
your smile wide from the thrill!

I remember

My mouth opens in amazement
as I watch from my seat, barely noticing
my ice-cold coke shaking in my hand!

You fly! you soar! you land on your feet!
raise your arms, take a bow, round of applause!
a dancer at the peak of her shine!

I remember

You skipped like your last words,
you leaped like your last heartbeat,
you stood out like a cancer.

I stare at the place you cartwheeled,
only my ice-cold cola for comfort,
the sun, once bright, dims like a dream.

## Gold, Bars

By Cameron Simpson

I'll take the gold, hold the bars.

So long as the money keeps flowing

The rest of you can have a different kind of golden stream.

## Gran's Custard

By Jay Rose Ana

In memories land of family lore, of pain and hardship, and more.
There lived a legendary custard maker, my sweet old Gran.
Her custard was a tantalising concoction
– one that could bring even the saddest of souls to joy.
Everyone knew, when Gran whipped out her trusty mixing bowl,
something magical was about to happen.
Gran's kitchen was a charming mess,
– like a mini-tornado had danced right through it.
Flour dusted countertops. Pots and pans danced precariously
– on hot stove rings.
It didn't matter, the heavenly aroma of warm custard was enough
– enough to make sense of chaos and other stuff.
One day, I decided to learn custard-making from Gran herself.
Armed with pencil, scrap of paper, and a good dose of enthusiasm,
I stood ready to be initiated into the custard-making society.
Seeing my enthusiasm, Gran winked mischievously and whispered,
"Ah, dearie, it's all in the wrist action!"
She stirred with a wooden spoon, as if some ancient custard sorcery.
I wouldn't be surprised if she mixed custard under light of moon.
As she mixed ingredients, flour rained from her bowl like confetti.
I managed to cover myself in a dusting of white,
gaining a hearty chuckle from Gran, "You're a natural!".
When the custard was ready, I eagerly scooped it into my mouth.
The taste was divine. Creamy, sweet, and filled with love.
It was as if happiness itself had been turned into a pudding.
From that day on, I was crowned Gran's custard apprentice.
We spent many afternoons together,
laughing and making a mess in her kitchen.
And though my custard never quite matched Gran's,
she always praised my efforts.
Awarding me title of Grand Custard Mistress.
Whenever I think of Gran, I can't help but smile.
And remember those custard-filled days.
The light she brought to darkness, with her grin and custard-y ways.

## She

By Freddie Barker

She gave me the gift of spring:
The fuzz of a honeybee – minus the sting;
She showed me elegance in golden things:
In the sun and the moon – but never diamond rings.

She said the yellow in life made gold seem unimpressive,
That kings with shining crowns were repulsively excessive.
That success in itself was less about having riches;
Because richness comes from feeling safe and butterfly stitches.

She paired daffodil petals with a daisy's heart,
Declared the fully-yellow flower as our best work of art.
She gave it to me to weave into her hair –
Bleach blonde – no-one was fond – but she never cared.

She was yellow. Not only happy - but radiant.
Crazily zany and rarely obedient.
Aware that life had a missing ingredient;
The search for joy is so simple, and fear so malignant.

She knew the colour of ducks' bills, sleeping pills,
and the cotton twills on her favourite dungarees
symbolised magnificence.

And now as I pull stray buttercups
from scrapbook pages that gather dust;
she: a forever treasure, an irreverent, benevolent, happy-go-lucky
sentiment; lights the room
as her memories
glow yellow.

## The Alchemist

By Damon Lord

Seeking, striving to change
Tear away the former life
From malleable, industrious lead
Heavy and burdened, shape imposed.
Evolve! into something beautiful
Transcend, transform, translate
A butterfly's magical chrysalis.
Always hidden before,
Assume the genuine form
Auric now, shining free!
Through gentle alchemy
You are accepted as precious gold.

## Yellow

By Niamh Baxter

Sunflowers grow facing the sun,
reaching up to the sky,
as golden rays cascade down onto them,
a warmth wrapping the body,
heating every fibre,
like a flickering flame twitching on the end of a match,
as it dances towards-
as it leans into-
the pale scattered power,
specks,
aflame.
The sulphur alight,
the sight-
growing.

As it darkens and twists and turns,
and there's a suffocating feeling,
scratching at your throat,
picking away at the skin,
chipping at the painted smile,
tearing the soft banana peel that cocoons you,
the flesh smashed between burnt thumbs,
as tears made of lemon juice drip into the rip at the nail,
oozing like honey, the sting worms its way to your core,

as the gas grows
and grows
and expands
and grows
and chokes you out-
amber alarms blaring out,

need to let out-

Sunflowers grow facing the sun,
reaching up to the sky,

or else the petals shrivel up,
turned sour, left to die,
in a weeping pile of rotting stems,
like a heart,
locked in a golden plated cage,
drowned out by a nauseating sea of yellow.

## Bare

By Zoe Dempsey Martínez

My friend likes to peel lemons.
They leave ringlets of streetlight on the counter,
Set their teeth to the tender sun born there,
And I think of how rare it is to see certain things shed their skin.

You're allowed to be citrus,
find where I bleed.
I'll draw a bath for you,
put a kettle to shimmer,

pour honey, brown sugar, molasses,
into every room that swims with acid,
or sprinkle soda till every counter glimmers.
Whatever you need.

What a rare thing,
to peel the waxy day away,
undress a softer sun of velvet and lace.
Filigree of citrine, let me see your face.

## Love Is A Sunflower

By Quinn Cross

Love is a sunflower, growing towards the sky.
The sun is a warm embrace and the rain is like tears.
Love is that sunflower growing nice and tall, a narrative of romance for us to all follow.
The seeds in the middle are the secrets that we keep.
Love is a sunflower shining on me.

Love is a sunflower, its colourings beam light and happiness.
Love is the sunflower, that follows the warm moments throughout the day and night.
Love pivots on a moment, hanging by a thread, but the sunflower uses that to its advantage.
Staying still and only moving its head, following the warmth of love.

Love is a sunflower, simple and plain but noticeable there if you take the time.
Love needs to be nurtured and fed as does the sunflower.
Love and sunflower can stand alone, but for how long before it crumbles and dies?

This is why I say love is a sunflower, don't disregard it.
Treasure all the moments the sunflower, the love can bring.
We never know how long it can last or when the next sunflower may arrive, but maybe one day this sunflower will turn out to be your groom or your bride.

## Trip

By Ian Parker Dodd

Her finger nails drew pictures on his skin

as lava lamps tumesced in red and green.

But switches tripped and water crowns

jazzed and span across a garden pond

and stained glass flashed yellow rain.

No blown fuse was found but she left

with heated oils to smooth another.

## The Yellow Rose Tree

By Ian Parker Dodd

*In 400 BCE Greek soldiers were drugged by azalea honey in pots*
*left by a roadside. The same thing happened to Roman soldiers in 60 BCE.*

It is a promiscuity of yellow flowers,

trussed on twigs, grey-bearded with lichen

these sun-burst pentagrams show slicks

like Jersey cream, streaming down their throats

Shadow lines bisect their other limbs. They twist

like lovers stretching from an embrace

whilst pollen shivers in a breeze

waiting on naked nectar seekers.

As sun turns to moon, a mad honey scent

viscous with narcosis, thickens with promise

## Lemon Curd

By Lisa Millard

"I like it thick, but not too thick,"

she used to say as she spread

a perfect quantity of strength

throughout her day

It was a little zing to bring her joy

a whipped shiny sunrise

that she could hide her troubles behind

Contrasting crunch as she bit

through the smooth spread

tongue popping with all the things

she should have said

Lemon curd was a choice she relished

embellishing her bread with a shiny jewel.

She chose to eat it whenever she dared

lemon curd was a choice

when so many others had been stripped bare

## Coffee Cake Communion

By Eleni Brooks

my body too broken to

go and receive His

it felt like I'd

missed out

til last night

a cake slice

preached the napkin-wrapped truth

this is Christ's body

broken for you

## Yellow, Now

By Laura Jane Round

I'm passing a sunlit deli by the sea
When you call my name.
Shock, first;
Then delight,
Genuine, frictioned delight when you
Pull me close,
Our waterproof coats embrace.
The smile dances the length and breadth
Of my salted lips, and ah
There's that pain again.
You have such lovely children.
My heart feels fragile now,
Swaddled in chip paper
Some talking, then
You fade light sea mist, like the spray of tide
Like the yellowed bruise,
The point of healing.

## All My Favourite Things Are Yellow- Except For You

By Rhi Armstrong

All my things are yellow.
My shoes, sometimes my hair,
my skin that one time I got sick
the notebooks that I doodle in.
My favourite flowers with their
heads tilted in search for light.
That childhood bear-
sticky, supple, sweet from honey.
The bunny that sits in my bed,
fur flat from sleepy cuddles.
Of course you would never know.
I bet you don't even remember
when I wanted to paint my walls yellow.
It was your place,
a fresh start for us.
The promise of not just weekend stay overs
in mould filled flats and dreary pubs and
sofa surfing where I always ended up on the floor.
And I wanted my walls yellow.
Wanted my walls to shine through
the thin cloudy line of cigarette smoke
and the smell of whiskey in the morning
I tell you I want yellow,
the sun glow on my skin,
the brightness of a future that I
can not even begin to imagine.
And you look at me disgruntled
because you are used to living
in cold, dark places.

IVY

## The School Field

By Niamh Baxter

He loves me,
he loves me not,
the fate of us left in the petals of a daisy,
one picked from the school field.

Grass tickles the back of my neck,
as I lie,
hidden away from the warm rays,
tucked under a tree in the corner of the school field.

Leaves fluttering,
stem held between dirt coated fingertips,
he loves me,
the white truths scattered across green,
he loves me not,
the chlorophyll stains my school dress,
scuffed shoes and pollen dusted nails.

Fate is decided,
only the blades of grass below,
and the fresh leaves above will know,
what the flower petals whispered to me that day,
lying down on the school field.

## Mown Grass Memories

By Eleni Brooks

summer smelt of tension

waiting to be touched

this year smells of tennis

John says *30 love*

## Serene Green

by Oly Bliss

My fingers drop into the space of your thumb and index finger
You are warm and strong

Two walls, two glass doors
Green paint reflecting gold
Frames our flow of living

One purring cat each,
Two hot water-bottles
Dual vinyl-players on repeat

Their rhythm
languid, content, sleeping
A pair of tiny hearts, beating

While you scroll, snooze, crochet or read
I draw, eat and play with beads

You like
Oat milk first, tea bag second,
Whilst I have;
A full pot of coffee,
Splash, of oat milk and maple
Instead of honey.

You routinely add decaf grains into the jar
To keep my heart

Safe and steady.

## A Frog Daydreams

By Janet Jenkins

I wish I could
be smooth instead of
gnarled. green and slimy,
have eyes in front of my head
(blimey, it isn't much to ask.)
Take a snooze in a feather bed
instead of mud and hollows.
I wish I could
speak softly to only one mate,
not croaking loudly for piggy-back rides.
I can't abide the constant squashing
and tossing away the competition.
I wish I could
dance with a princess who'll change
my life with a kiss. Have a sweet, giggly,
baby; the wiggly ones I won't miss.
I wish I could
sit on a sofa with my lover holding
a glass of wine as we watch the rain;
take pity on my former mates
who can't wait to escape
from their soggy, samey lives

## Sub La Verda Stelo (Under The Green Star)

By Damon Lord

A language's green star flag unfurled.
A dream to communicate across the world.
Esperanto, a vision vast and grand:
Enthusiasts united from every land.
Yet global reach an impossible quest,
But in speakers' hearts, it came to nest.
Community thriving, hope planted, strong,
Celebrating differences in life's song.
Beneath this verdant banner, friendships sown
Through a cherished tongue, amity grown.

Flugu, verdstela flago de la lingvo.
Revu: komuniki ĝoje en monda ringo.
Esperanto, la celo vasta, kaj granda:
Entuziasmuloj kunigitaj el ĉiu lando.
La mondon tamen ne eblas konkeri la peto,
Sed en koroj de parolantoj fariĝis nesteto.
Espero planita, komunumo floranta,
Festante vivdiferencojn per harmonio kanta.
Sub ĉi tiu verdverda standardo, amikeco semata
Per ĉies amata lingvo, amikeco kreskata.

## Jade Green Dragoness

Laura Liptrot

Once upon a time, when gods walked the earth,

A she made of water: bones ice cold jade,

Lived upon the world – predated its birth –

A dragon; the mother: mankind she made;

And man made gods retreat into the sky.

Revenge was sought out: the gods did conspire,

To trick the dragoness (that she may die);

To shed her godly cloak and taste desire:

A mortal man was made to make her fall,

Into a love so deep that she may drown;

A mortal woman, without power at all,

The people burned her spirit: cut her down.

Her flesh became the rivers; and her bones:

They scattered to the earth as jade green stones.

## Half Sage And Half You

By Lauren Frankland

prozac on your nightstand,
half sage and half cream,
yet the sweetness comes from you
and the normalcy of our morning routine.
because the calm in the storm,
here is where I belong,
yet after all this frustration,
i find my peace within your arms.
'doctor doctor! it hurts when i do this-'
'so don't do it?' you say,
then stifle me with a kiss
as my worries melt away, and i feel safe again.
the light streams in,
as your alarm goes off,
and the way you say good morning
in a voice so sleepy and soft
half sage and half cream,
the sweetness is still you,
as i reach, half asleep,
to the prozac sitting on your nightstand,
counting my blessings because you're you.

## Paint The World Green

By DK

We gotta paint the world green
If you know what I mean
Climate change is real, it ain't no joke
Time to take action, let's ignite the smoke

Gotta break the chains, let's break the mould
Mother Earth needs us, we gotta be bold
No more pollution, no more greed
It's time to take action and plant the seed

People feeling contact burns off the pavement
Climate change got us feeling so complacent
Sustainable living, it's the way to be
Protecting our Earth, for you and me

Plant-based diet, fuelling our bodies, feeling alive
No more harming animals, it's time to thrive
From the forests to the oceans, we gotta strive
To keep the earth's beauty, gotta keep it alive

From the concrete jungles to the rolling hills
Let Mother Nature heal, let her spirit be filled
With the colours of green, the beauty of life
Let's strive for a future that's free from strife

No more deforestation, no more devastation
We gotta change our ways, time for revelation
Reduce our carbon footprint, make it a sensation
Together we can make a difference, no hesitation

About the changes we're making, the steps we take
To ensure a future for generations at stake
It's time to be woke, open our eyes
To the impact we have, no more denying the skies
We gotta educate, spread the word far and wide
About the importance of living with the earth in mind
Veganism, it's more than just a fad
It's a lifestyle choice, a way to make a stand
Against factory farming, animal cruelty
Choosing compassion, living consciously

## Nettles

By Chaz Jubin

I've never been stung by a bee
Or a wasp, thankfully
Never a Hornet
But I've been stung by nettles
Again and again
Over and over
And when I'm getting over
The last sting
The past pain
I inevitably get stung again
Mindlessly on a walk
I'll stroll into a bush
And it stops my talk
Unable to yell
I'm not allowed to complain
It's so frequent now

## List Of Green Creatures In My Childhood Bedroom

By Zoe Dempsey Martínez

A stolen book of crosswords, half done, none finished.

A frog with a soft fuzzy pelt, the size of the first dog that bit me.

My adolescent heart, stirring in a toybox.

A bowl of grapes by my bedside, decadent, store bought.

Patches on a duvet, windows of meadow lime sky.

A copy of Othello, a green-eyed monster stalking its ribbed back,
claw marks through the dust dunes of my shelves.

The hands of a boy, rotting in a sock drawer.

The floor I forgot about, sleeping cool marble,
witness of twenty years of things spilled.

## The Stem

By Ellie Dart

It'll carry envy through itself,
pulling red root into colour.
hold heavy, rainbow sun
and wait for a snapshot

synthesised glow that blooms a mixed pallet.
You'll find yourself within a tulip,
tucked, trying to grow through
the wind and soft petal husks
to rupture its skin sheet into being.

## Green-Eyed Monster

By Natalie Carr

I look at her with longing,
I want the life she leads,
I get excited when she fails,
And angered when she succeeds.
I wonder if I can take it all,
And leave her in the dust,
Because to see this girl in my shoes,
Essentially is a must.

I know I have the monster,
Green eyed, perched upon my shoulder,
And the more I believe I can succeed,
My actions get even more bolder.

I wait until she is alone,
To humiliate and torment,
She is up there in my head,
Living there without paying rent.

And I vent that life's not fair,
That this girl gets everything I want,
And that the universe should favour me,
In my endeavours for once.

So, I set her up for the win,
Infront of all her peers,
I know she'll feel accepted,
And that this will quell any fears.

And as she stands there on the stage,
About to give her speech,
The lever that I need to pull,
Not so far out of reach,
I pull it, and over her head,
The pig's blood spills all over,
And at last, I've had revenge,

I've finally got my closure.

But then what happens next,
Takes me by surprise,
Because the girl is special,
And can move shit with her eyes.

And she has her eyes set on me,
My chances of escape I'm trying to tally,
Cause I just made an enemy,
Of that weirdo in my school called Carrie.

## The Enchanted Forest

By Ade Couper

The air was fresher here.

Outside, thick sweaty air laid over the land
Like an over-thick duvet on a summer night,
Whilst here, there was a freshness.

Hardly-seen birds fluttered and frolicked,
Their movements half-seen, tracked
By the rustle of the foliage.

Sounds hinted at the movements
Of mightier beings:
Wild Boar? Red Deer?
Maybe even Herne himself...

Move deeper.
The almost-sound, more a sense
Of running water tells of a river here.
Move deeper, downward, toward.

The feel of the forest changes,
As if it, and those within
Have been removed from mere linear time.
Go on.

The trees.
Hundreds of years of life- maybe more-
Etched into the ragged cragged bark.
These trees may well have seen
Dragons, knights, seers, wizards,

Would that they could talk
Or sing their ancient songs...

Senses are muddled here.
Some of these trees look
More than just trees-
There is a feeling that,
Any moment now,
These trees will look, move, talk.
A fancy, surely? Maybe,
But these are the old lands,
We are the interlopers here...

## Matcha

By Zoe Dempsey Martínez

I buy a matcha latte
at the queer café
dig for pennies at
the yawning yard of May

sell my heart for anything
that brings me back to hills
and the winking light of canopies
that bleed green on windowsills

my left eye for the clink of ice
and a quiet place to stay
my right eye for soft gay singing
and a tall glass of matcha latte

## Dragoning

By Rhi Armstrong

There is no room for sorrow
in a heart full of fire.
Maybe that's why I wanted to be a dragon.
Not for the fame,
not for the fable.
I have always heard how
they are slain by men,
false knights of greed and vice
and I know now that dragons are
not some furious beast,
some monster murdering innocent peace
but rather dragons are women
no longer oppressed.
No longer slotted in categories,
not dressed to impress.
Dragons are a sisterhood,
unbound by earth,
unbound by man,
unbound by womanly pain.
Skin falling away like old petals,
Scales of emerald in their place
taking the warmth through their scales
as they flutter to the skies
which smells of something beginning.
I shall be a shadow streaking across the sky-
fleeting, speeding and utterly gone.

## Esther Who Thinks That, Even If I Eat My Greens, I'll Still Rot In Hell

By James Mason

She used to say the most ridiculous things
and I'd agree because I wanted to sleep with her.
She once said food shouldn't be green.
And suddenly that night as I listened
to her pull the vowels out of her mouth
like a string of glistening, wet chewing gum,
(greeeeeeeeeen, she said, her face ruffled
with disgust but sounding pleased with itself)
I didn't want to sleep with her anymore.
What a petty little monster I seemed to myself
as I squeezed through the narrow window
in the restaurant's loos then vaulted the back fence.
(Not brave enough to stiff Esther for the bill, I'd slipped
a twenty down the front of the Maître D's shirt
to cover her rum and cokes and my crème de menthe.)
Alone in bed, I pressed down hard on where it hurt:
some pea-sized, over-boiled and pedantic lump
that had snarked asparagus, grapes, haricot verts.

## The Death of Mint

By L. E. Wynn

My partner bought a mint plant from Morrisons.
He wants to be more sustainable, eco-green
As the leaves in the cradle of his hands.

He wants to begin a flower-pot herb garden
in our kitchen to negate the concrete
car park outside our front door,
hopes it will distract from the dual carriageway
where our actual garden should be.

He nurtures it, tells it compliments and jokes
as he waters the soil, apologises when he plucks
a few leaves he needs to cook with.

After a few short weeks, it rots and dies,
flies having nested somewhere in its stem.
He holds a little funeral for it, laying it gently
in the bottom of our bin.

Eventually the lack of nature becomes a running joke,
whenever we shop, we gesture to plants and whisper
that would be nice in our garden that we definitely have.

I notice how he looks at the herbs but
walks away before I suggest trying again.
I'll wait for the day he walks towards them.

## Bio-Growth

By Ash Bainbridge

pip
swells to
earth-root bulb /
squaring jaw bor-
ders sprout tache-stem shoots /
pores / saltily enriched
by aura clouds / bloom / stretch / joints
burn with flash-cool gelled air-dried feeds /
hip planters grind / primed for tumble weeds
down curled trails while height climbs to squared edges

## Hiding Behind 3 R's:

By Quinn Cross

Save the resources,
Recycle they say.
But the environment they claim to be saving,
Is just a game for them to play.

They put it up in a wish bottle and hang it on the wall.
Hoping the problem would soon just fall.
Melt away, not exist.
But leave it there, they've missed the trick.

Like a worn out map,
They needed a slap,
When the polar ice caps started to melt,
They finally decided they needed to do something else.

"Recycling. That's what we need." One guy shouted.
Echoes of "Hear! Hear!" filled the room.
Until one of those wise chappies chirped up
"What does recycling actually do?"

None of them seemed to have a clue.
Until one day one of them said
"Back to recycling, good egg.
For I have a plan. We cleanse and reuse it."

Nods and cheers were had by all.
They flew planes,
They had a ball.
Knowing that their world was saved.

Recycling.
Their hero.
Nothing else needed to be done.
Hiding their sins behind 3 R's.

Reduce. Reuse. Recycle.
Surely we could do more?

## Ilona Nescia

By Robin Cain

The moss follows
Our footsteps marked by
Mother Nature's memory
Long lost is the dents of
Soft soil.
It has been trained
In the pillowy footsteps of
The damned
The depressed
The mournful
But not for those that live
Underneath.
Instead, themselves,
For the days without you
Last longer.
Life shorter.
Colder.
Grieving bodies hunched
Aching with love
In the steep of tabor
Winds grace my being
Being swept away
Into the gallows
Not even six feet
Will tarnish you
Oh, Love of mine
Mist is the sheet that covers
The face
A ghost I become
So hollow and pale
In the natural dull of these valleys
I am with you
I want to pray
To listen to her
To hear her voice once again.
Witnessing her four-foot figure

Cardigan wool melting
As she wanders through
her deep mahogany and sage canopy.
To her heavenly gaze
A biscuit to be offered and refused
But she'll leave you one anyway.
Snow white curls falling
Graciously with ease
in these bordered memories

haunt me
lace my mind
with the image of pure love
for she is a mighty force
that pulls me closer to her.
A pain of missing
A life I do not live
In these terrains of tender leaves
Grass unscathed
My blood is here
In these grounds
I spill everywhere to be with you
Fernweh for you tabor.
For here with her
I will lay.

## Nature's Call

By Ash Cascavilla

Save us.
Save us.
Save us.

We are one.
Moss, weeds, flowers, and algae.
We will be gone soon.
You have not helped us so far,
Do it now
Stop the pesticides and chemicals,
Reduce your nasty pollution,
Think before you doom us all.

We are your one chance,
Don't let us go.
We beg you.
We are older and wiser than you.
We do not deserve your tortures.

If we die, you do too.
Don't make that mistake.
Cherish us before we are gone.
Look at our beauty and colours.
Love our powers,
the oxygen we give you.
They are superior to yours.
We can endure without you, but you can't.

## Foam

By Freddie Barker

I mixed absinthe with fairy liquid.

Each bubble bursts with pungent scented anaesthetic:

I'm numbed by
dizzy spells and fizzy apple
betwixt
ancient manuscripts,
lucid dreams
and dissonance.

& glycerine strands paint hieroglyphs onto the dishes.

## Seabed

By Robin Cain

Tidal waves gentle but stubborn
Carry this weight submerged by the subconscious
The everchanging settlement of deepness
A symphony of sounds and light
showers of clouds brought me
back here to present
Yourself to me
Struggling through a thickness of serenity
I fought life to show me myself
But you stood in front of me
Instead
In a rich teal scene
But it suited you
In ways I couldn't say aloud
But it encapsulated me
To say you were there
Looking into me
With your ocean vastness
and intimate meadow sky
under luminescent pops
I watch myself attach to you
Under this blanket of the seabed

FORGET
- ME -
NOT

## Hurricane

By Liam Brabbing

With a simple exhale
A hurricane was born
A disaster of
My own making
Creeping across the skies, swallowing up
Earth and air alike
Burying it's claws along the mainland
Rampaging over everything
I can't relax because
Every cyclone
Every eruption
It's always been me
I am the eye of the storm
And the lightning
The man who thunders

## Blue With Blue

By Ian Parker Dodd

Her eyes were black eyed Susans.
Cornflower blooms, rose petals
made nosegays round her throat.

Come in she said I'll give you refuge
from the rage, let my dye indigo
soften thickened skin — unloosed

her aizome kimono tattooed morning
glory bell on my keloid brands
married them to her scarred woad

and bouquets tied to broomsticks,
we flew moon rainbows to the sun.

## Stargazing At Dawn

By Cameron Simpson

Starlight shimmer, join the dots
One-two-three in black and white

Ursa Major, Ursa Minor
Hercules, Ophiuchus, Lyra

Cloudless skies at four ay em,
Lie back and watch the heavens dance
Cepheus and Cassiopeia
Perseus, Pegasus, Andromeda

Morning dew on soft grass-down
Sleeping silent, vacant lots

Gemini and Aires, Leo
Cancer, Scorpius, Libra, Virgo

Hand-me-down binoculars
Recounting myths of millennia past

Orion, Cygnus, Boötes, Lepus
Draco, Hydra, Eridanus
The black and white gives way to blue
Watch the sunrise

## Dirge For A Fallen Thunderbox

By Damon Lord

Little rank plastic cabin casualty
Prone, on your side.
Victim of a violent assault by night.
In the murderous morning,
Solemn construction workers gather round,
Mourning their portable toilet,
Reeking place of respite.
Blue fetid essence stains
Creeping o'er the spoiled path
Draining away putrid chemicals into the gutter.
After the work is done, after all is gone
The putrid azure scar lingers
Remembering the spot where you surrendered.

## The Pigeon

By Freddie barker

Her tail feathers
refract
Hints of heather; a heavenly
solace she
perches, daintily.

Among torn receipts
and shards of glass
her nest is woven between sheets of chiselled concrete.

Smoke drifts beyond a rain-stained
storm drain

a dedicated
mother
of pearl,
she cradles
a shining egg
between her feet.

Her feathers, a plumed ruffle
a stark softness
in a sleepless city:
a catacomb of turbulence.

She is faint, painted periwinkle;
merely a spec of ash within a tectonic network of
industry, motion, exhaust, and clamour.

She, a silhouette of defencelessness,
her plea - a gentle coo - is symphonic.

## As The World Implodes

By Niamh Baxter

Grab your closet friend,
right then and there and ask them to dance.
Lavender lights swirl around you,
whisk away your blue tinted memories,
everyone will be forgotten anyway,
left to this space,
anything and nothing and everything,
gentle heartache laces those lips that break into a fit of laughter,
as everything fractures
and trickles down like raindrops
hitting your face,
puddles forming at your feet,
take the hands,
tender and cracked and fading,
stained with a hidden sadness,
and dance it all away.
The floor swept under tapping feet,
and you laugh,
eyes sparkling with an unknown understanding,
sapphire blush coating your cheeks,
a single crack in your front tooth
tears of memories wiped away,
gone.
Yesterday is gone,
tomorrow is no more,
flesh to ash,
body disintegrates,
our minds drifting,
dancing,

as the word implodes.

## Fusion

By Susan Wood

Sense the heat,
Russet dust on fingertips
Coned vision tunnels upwards

*Alchemist fuses*
*Scavo, silica, sand*

Volcanic blow of cinnamon pulse-beat
Congealing quartz and blast,
Searing swelter bellows

*Alchemist incants-*
*Crucible, calliper, cullet*

Glory-hole, annealer,
Mouth-blown organism breathes,
Steel blow-pipe branding

*Alchemist transforms*
*Molten, marver, murrini*

Calefaction, furnace pit,
Chemical steam and smoke-
Augery of livid creation

*Alchemist conjures*
*Calliper, cullet, rondelle*

Singe of water,
Gathering iron, cane,
All-seeing glass-maker's chair

*Alchemist enchants*
*Teardrop, fluted, crystal-*

*Glass.*

## How Was Your Morning?

By Eleni Brooks

I said, *do you want me to answer honestly?*

You said, *I want you to tell me*

*everything*. Sometimes you are just like God.

I love my lines for Healthy Minds, but with you

I am unscripted, addicted to the peace that comes

from the passenger side. While you drive

we talk about my pain and Jesus.

You say, *The fullness of God* means He never leaves us;

Two hours ago I'd have disagreed but

I'm learning that a table in the presence of my enemies

can be a bacon sandwich after suicidal fantasies.

## A Hue Of Blue

by Mx. Adam Khan

**Tantalising(ly)** the senses, I succumb
**Vivid** blue hues
**As** plenty as the rainbow spectrum
**None** of them giving me the blues
**Sky** blue has immense views
**Sightings** over the horizon
**Turquoises** which we cruise
**To(o)** the melody of the rolling waves
**Deep** navy blues that bemuse
**Down** along the cold currents
**Bright** violets which accuse
**Borders** blue yet worthy
**Azure** permeating fields where they transfuse
**Allures** those who seek floral scents
**Cobalt** from the deep earth muse
**Cold** to the taste and touch
**Midnight** blue from the far flung amuse
**Masses** of space to lead to the dark
**Teal** so delicately paired with chartreuse
**Touched** upon ceramics ever so slightly
**Indigo** as you snooze
**Ideations** formed you close your eyes
**Cyan** as fresh as breaking news
**Spectral** purity to create colour
**Many** more hues interfuse
**Blues** which I could choose

## Bystander Blues

By Zoe Dempsey Martínez

They say imagine the train tracks,
and suddenly there's the train.
Faces pressed under gilded glass like blue monarchs,
steam rolled out like white dough under the stubborn thumb
of the stratosphere.

They say imagine a switch.

There's a spot for you here,
a seat by the tracks.
The wind the train tows sows through your bones
and births you as a wheat field.

They say imagine your hand outstretched.
A lit match swelling with solitude
Sprouting from your shoulder an infant blue flame.

They say imagine her on the tracks.
And you're a child learning how
Trains cut through field and flesh
And how bruises burst forth from choice.

## Clear Mind

By M. Viswak Senudu

Free of thoughts and clear mind,
Now I'll not look behind.

No space for trauma and tears anymore,
Let me untie myself and freely explore.

I'm immersed in my own company,
acquainted to myself,

Realising no need of anyone.
From now no sleepless nights,

Under the moon lights.

## My Thoughts Before The Hearing

By Freddie Barker

Yes?
Or no comment?
A glint of desperation matches mine
in the bathroom mirror.

A peppermint mouthwash spritz.
a lagoon of lilac spit
gathers in the sink,

and I think,
sterile - or fresh?

The fluid in my spine
compresses
jumbled bones
and mangled flesh

I feel brittle.
And I bite down on my toothbrush.

## Hot Blood

By Ash Cascavilla

Vessels of life.
Red for the fight
Blue for the vitality
We channel the negative products out
All the excesses that you don't need,
Pumping through our blue channels
Of pure blue vein life.
The lungs don't beg for air
They plead for the blood to be renewed
And CO2 to be removed
So that we can exist a moment longer.

Blue is life
Each living person posses veins
To free themselves of negativity
Physical and metaphorical.
All to fight the red hot reality
With a cool dark blue
That bellies the true power it wields.

## An Excerpt From Kashala Abrahams' Dissertation 'Herneith And Sabu' Based On William Shakespeare's 'Macbeth.'

By Kashala Abrahams

"Our child had died inside of me again and to etch the occasion, the Gods torn the lapis lazuli blue sky in shards and scattered the translucent petals across the earth—we sat in our large, ivory home in thunder, lightning, and in rain."

## The New Man In My Neighbourhood

By Quinn Cross

They said he was evil but now he's good.
He recently came to my neighbourhood.
I'm wary of that big blue brained brute.
That Megamind in his brand new suit.

His only friend is a robot with a fish for a head.
He used to not care who turned up dead.
But now he's changed down to his soul,
I hope he has no other goal.

Maybe blue won't be as scary,
If I talked with him most fairly.
I did just that, he seemed quite nice.
Maybe we'll be friends for life.

## Royal Robes

By Sage White-Drake

There they are!
Hail the Monarch so Regal and wise.
By grace of a deity given this kingdom.

Let's move away from politics and ideology and into fashion.

Those robes!
Those robes!

Silky
Soft
Deep
Rich
Furry

I bet they're like wearing a cloud.
Being wrapped in silk, velvet or ermine sounds nice.

You can keep the power, keep the wealth, keep the throne.

Just give me the ROBE!

## Tchaikovsky's Swan Racecourse

By L. E. Wynn

Odette stares from the centre
of a flooded, semi-frozen racecourse.
I catch her gaze and hold it close,
eager to watch her ballet.

She is a picture-perfect painting to be framed,
hung above a fireplace as winter-kissed fingers thaw,
a blink-and-you'll-miss-it detail in a film you saw.
She is the stillness
of an audience waiting
for a performance to start.

Odette turns and glides away, decides not
to play her part. She is tired of being seen,
heads for the horizon and finds
the vanishing point.

I wait for an orchestra that never plays.

## By The Light Of Blue Candles

By Ian Parker Dodd

Unzipped in blue with coffee cooled

our bodies moved as if in grooves.

But unwarmed by smoking wicks

our mouths spewed ropes of curdled air,

made static hum, unravelled

bedridden you and stood up me.

## Blessed Are The Bluey Watchers

By Eleni Brooks

lift-the-flap to find

2 girls, a dragon

a corner sofa

& a one-of-a-kind show.

## My Favourite Place To Be

By Rhi Armstrong

Foam clouds lapse through the darkness,
as though the earth's ceiling has collapsed
to the ground and
we dance through it.
The air tinged with
salt spray in my face,
it is bitter yet we are gleeful.
Tide full, lapping at our feet as
we jump the waves.
We will age like sea glass,
shaped shiny by the rough of life.
Hard edges glazed over
You wash away the sand from my skin,
catching the waves in your hands,
the talents of Poseidon in your palms.
Tomorrow,
the 'love yous' etched into the sand
will be carried off to a different land,
far away from here.
But right now, we are kids
building ice cream castles and dreams
and kissing to Valarie.

## A Lavender Sprig

By Robin Cain

A lavender sprig picked
To adorn your attire
I fix your tie
and pin the sprig
to your blazer pocket
it was always her favourite
you were the one to tell me.
late summers day,
to shepherd's night
washing up watching the
sun peak away behind the trees
a cascade of blanket blushing clouds
we were taking her in from the kitchen
how she was pruning and potting
pondering on that pillowy bed of
wild lilacs
enjoying her evening routine of plucking
the perfect indigo
placing under her head
her preferred nights rest.
Letting them dry hung from the sky
or what it seemed when I was chair height
"if you do this they won't die"
She told me in our secret escapades
of life caring for those pockets of mauve delight.
I still find them now in tired coats and worn wallets
Even in my bright magenta barbie dreamhouse
As she sneaks her way back to me once in a while
Unannounced but completely enamoured
She is still here.
One last look, over the sprig on your pocket
"don't worry I've got her safe"
My grandfather's words rang true
Stepping through the church doors,
She always hated when we wore black.

## Forget-Me-Not

By Chaz Jubin

This is not a goodbye,
Death ended a life but not the relationship,
We'll look back on memories, precious
Provoke nostalgia of you still here
Remember the good and the bad,
It is what makes us human.
This is not a farewell.
You left to avoid the rush as they say
For now,
We'll see you in the roses,
The smell of freshly cut grass,
In the smiles, laughs and even the tears,
Your immeasurable beauty, found in friends and family.
This is not an Adieu.
The ripples you caused keep going,
Glittering around us in the oceans of affection
You may not be here but your memory is
It's in the stars at night,
The Sunsets during the day,
Cups of tea every hour
And your love passed down
In generations.
This is 'see you again'.
There is love in holding on,
But there is love in letting go.
No rules written to guide you,
Free to go on your journey
One we hope to meet you on
Once we've finished here too
See you Soon, I love you.

# COLOUR THEORY

Authors

## Ade Couper

Ade Couper has been writing and performing poetry since about 2017; he was the Worcestershire Poet Laureate 2021-22, and has been published in several anthologies. Ade's debut collection Made of Stories was published this year by Black Pear Press. Ade has been an activist for human rights & disability rights for longer than he cares to admit to: his hobbies include annoying his younger work colleagues by going on about the good old days when you didn't have to input everything onto computers. His ambition in life is to be Captain Mainwaring.

## Amelie Simon

Amelie Simon is often found cross-legged on floors of train stations writing about selfhood and devouring Wikipedia articles. She holds the title of Young Worcestershire Poet Laureate in 2023-24.

## Ash Bainbridge

Ash Bainbridge is a queer writer, former English teacher, and future midwife based in Worcester, UK. For Ash, language is safety, progress, and glue. Their creative process involves punchy re-re-re-drafts with vocab gifts from their unschooled children. In 2022, Ash received full mentorship with The Word Association, and their poems are published by – amongst others – Spoonie Press, The Winnow, Bleeding Thunder, and Solstice Literary Magazine. Ash's first chapbook Trans-crip-t, which explores their lived experiences as a trans non-binary menstruator with endometriosis and PMDD, is forthcoming with Bent Key Publishing in 2024.

## Ash Cascavilla

Ash is studying history and creative writing, moving into their last year of university. They love writing stories and poems a like with a fantastical touch to them. They also have an interest nature and the protection of that space.

## Ashley Whitehouse

Ashley is a poet who recently came runner up in his category for the Worcestershire LitFest: Young Writers competition. He is a dark minded, talented person with a love of nerdy things. They started writing poetry after their sibling recommended it to them as a way of venting their feelings and thoughts but discovered a hidden passion for the wondrous world of writing. Through writing, Ash and their sibling have been introduced to a community of loving and supportive people. Community & family are important to Ash, who knows that family doesn't end with blood.

## Brian Comber

Brian Comber lives in Worcestershire and writes poetry. He's performed at spoken word events in Worcester for many years and has had poems accepted for online publication with a variety of journals. He finds walking helps when he's stuck. Brian has had three poetry books published; Preparing a Child for the Physical World with Cerasus poetry together with Panopticon and (in 2023) A Caparisoned Elephant with Black Pear Press.

## Bryoney Cook

Bryoney Cook is a Scottish poet and an Independent Celebrant based in Birmingham, UK. She has participated in spring 2023's Apples and Snakes: Red Sky Sessions, and been spotlighted Poet by Very Rascals in December 2022, as well as taking part in regular West Midlands-based open mics. When not writing poetry, Bryoney spends her time writing non-traditional, love filled wedding and naming ceremonies for couples and families as a celebrant, in addition to her role in mental health engagement.

## Cameron Simpson

When he isn't drawing, animating or scriptwriting, Cameron writes poetry as a hobby alongside his degree. He likes poems that flow, with a strong rhythm and interesting visuals and metaphors, and takes maybe a little too much inspiration from his late-night daydreaming. Hopefully you enjoy reading his poems as much as he enjoyed writing them!

## Carriad Morgana

Carriad writes poetry from her own brutally honest perspective as a divorcee and member of the LGBTQ+ community. Having performed a hilariously funny poem for local dignitaries and Sophie Wessex, there's evidence to suggest she can laugh sometimes. Carriad volunteers and works at Worcester University for IMPACT and other universities. Having survived homelessness and severe depression, life is definitely worth living.

## Cat Whitehouse

Cat moved to Worcester in 2021 and is about to start their MA in Politics at Birmingham. She loves drama, musical theatre, D&D and all things nerdy! She is a part of Drama Queens Theatre Co. and recently performed at Saucy @ The Fringe. You can find her at Sugar Daddy's Café in Worcester - just look out for the purple hair!

## Chaz Jubin

Chaz is a down-to-earth person inspired by dark and twisty, experiences with family, and the simple things in life. They are a film and media student at University of Worcester and hope to become a college teacher one day, to inspire the next generation. Their poems, 'Forget-Me-Not' and 'Warm Marmalade', are dedicated to their grandparents Anne and Bea (Nanny Mint.)

## D.D. Holland

D. D. Holland is a novelist, poet and short story writer based in Gloucestershire. Holding a 1st Class BA in Creative Writing from the University of Worcester, D is now studying an MA at the University of Chichester. D is the winner of the V-Press Prize for Poetry and the Black Pear Press Prize for Fiction in 2022.

## Damon Lord

Damon Lord is Worcestershire Poet Laureate 2023/24. A writer of fiction and poetry, he is originally from Wales. He lives in Worcester with his wife and child. Damon speaks numerous languages, and is currently finishing a Master's degree in Creative Writing with the University of Hull. When not writing or reading, he can be found growing potatoes and carrots in his garden.

## DK

DK is a multi-faceted individual passionate about promoting inclusivity and equality for all. As an asexual, feminist, vegan living with cerebral palsy, he values the importance of representation and advocacy. Playing powerchair football and coaching the development team for Villa Rockets, he also strives to empower individuals with disabilities. Through the founding of AccessAbility Arts, DK is committed to making ALL art accessible, by creating a space where diversity and inclusivity are celebrated. His activism promotes unity and diversity for everyone.

## Eleni Brooks

Eleni is an autistic poet and a 23-24 vice chair of Worcester's Poetry Society, currently studying English Literature and Creative Writing at the university. Her work often focusses on her experiences of disability, religion, and sexual abuse. Lighter themes include her love of books, James Acaster, and the colour pink.

## Ellie Dart

Ellie Dart is a Worcestershire-based poet and previously held the title of Worcestershire Young Poet Laureate. In her final year at University of Worcester, she dedicated her time to the Poetry Society as a Vice Chair. After graduating with a degree in Literature and Creative Writing, Ellie now continues to write and perform at various poetry events.

## Freddie Barker

Freddie is a multimedia powerhouse: during her film production degree, she dedicates her energy to coordinating new events, workshops, fundraisers, and opportunities for students. Notable examples include founding and curating SPEAK VOLUMES! – a World Poetry Day celebration; contributing to the student-run Poetry Society committee from 2022-2024; advocating for poetry as rehabilitation through creative expression, and leading the assembly of this anthology!

## Hayden Robinson

Hayden Robinson is an autistic English writer and poet living in Decatur, GA. Many of his works focus heavily on neurodivergent experiences, and he is currently writing two horror novels, one about vampires and the other about living dolls. His works are in various publications such as Diverse Verse 3, Poetic Vision, Under the Fable and Mothmaw Anthology. During 2023, he published a short story Idolising Rebekah Kara and an article for Re-Route Art Magazine; he also published poetry for HNDL magazine.

## Ian Parker Dodd

Ian Parker Dodd was first published in Agenda in 1962. A great silence followed until 2016 when his wife died. The muse returned and he has read his work at both the Cheltenham and Ledbury festivals and at various open mics. His collection All they will call you published in 2021 has raised money for GARAS (Gloucestershire Action for Refugees and Asylum Seekers). He has also been published in several anthologies, the latest one being the Herefordshire Stanza groups anthology, Myths and Mysteries of Hereabouts, published in 2023.

## James Mason

James Mason has, in small and superficial ways, been a poet, editor and comedian. His most recent work appears in The Phare, Horla and Flash Fiction Magazine, as well as competition anthologies by Retreat West, Creative Mind and Cranked Anvil. His work also features in the 2021 and 2022 Worcester LitFest books. He has a Masters in Creative Writing.

## Janet Jenkins

Janet is a retired Nursery Headteacher from Hednesford who enjoys writing, gardening, and visiting theatre. Janet is leader of The Lichfield Poets and enjoys performing at festivals and events with group members. She reads at open mic events in Staffordshire and the West Midlands. She has poetry in several anthologies including Maligned Species and Diversifly (Fair Acre Press) Eighty Four (Verve Poetry Press) and In the Sticks (Offa's Press).

## Jay Rosa Ana

Jay Rose Ana lives in Worcester in the UK but exists mostly online through her YouTube Channel, A Leaf Falls, although she may occasionally be seen in the coffee queue at spoken word events. She explores the world from her laptop and writes her words through lived experiences, a deep soul, copious amounts of cake, and a fondness for words. Her debut collection of written poetry, Whispers in the Wind, was released in 2022.

## Jenny Hope

Jenny is a writer, poet, and woman with a tree thing. She lives on a hill in wildish Worcestershire – just on the cusp of the Herefordshire border. She's been published in small-press magazine, had a poetry collection published and read at Ledbury Poetry Festival as one of the V's. She is working on a fiction trilogy based on climate change and our changing landscapes.

## Kashala Abrahams

Kashala Abrahams is a Creative Writing and Screenwriting graduate from the University of Worcester who works in marketing. She's a business owner, and founder of The Marketing Vampire, (so watch out for your necks at night). Kashala volunteers for Journey to Justice, a social justice charity and is passionate about mental health inclusivity. She believes Kendrick Lamar is on the same scale as William Shakespeare, and she is deeply in love with spoken word poetry.

## L. E. Wynn

L. E. Wynn is an author and illustrator from the Black Country, West Midlands. They are a two-time University of Worcester graduate, earning a First Class Degree in Creative Writing and Illustration in 2022, and a PGCE in Secondary Art and Design in 2023. They are a former Poetry Society member, acting as Secretary for the 2021-2022 committee, where they organised and hosted weekly workshops. They have had poetry published with Dear Reader, and cover illustrations with JADEN magazine, Dark Thirty Publishing, and independent authors.

## Laura Jane Round

Laura Jane Round is a writer and performance poet from the Black Country in the West Midlands. They are the Editorial Director for Tenebrous Texts, a Liverpool John Moores alumni and a tea drinker over coffee. Their sophomore pamphlet, TEATH, was released by Alien Buddha Press in 2022.

## Laura Liptrot

Laura began her writing career at the age of 10, and after a hiatus of over a decade, began writing semi-professionally in 2017. She is a playwright and a poet and her passion for the written word was reignited by a couple of writing modules on her drama course at the University of Worcester. She seeks, through her poetry, to inspire others to find the very best in themselves and in the universe; to fight and win battles against negativity and to transform the ugly into the tremendously beautiful. Every story is precious. Every story is unique.

## Lauren Frankland

Lauren Frankland is a freelance creative and computing student at the University of Worcester. She has a great interest in dance, being a tap captain for the Dance Society in 22-23. She also enjoys scrapbooking. Her poetry tends to explore themes with emotions and random everyday objects, merging both her scientific and creative sides to craft unique and exciting poetry that often mimics the turbulence of day-to-day life.

## Liam Brabbing

Liam is a Worcester student who enjoys writing poetry as a unique means to express himself and has been doing so for a few years. Liam has evolved this hobby into a passion, expanding his work to include more emotion and subtle themes. After years of writing have honed his skills, he hopes to share his work more as he continues to progress and perfect his style.

## Lisa Millard

Lisa is a poet from the Midlands whose work usually reflects her passion of advocating for women's and animal rights. She also writes short stories some of which have been published in anthologies such as Small Leaf Press. Lisa's poem, Black Swan, won last year's Staffordshire LitFest and she is also a slam finalist. When she's not writing, Lisa also runs an animal sanctuary called Duckingham Palace.

## M. Viswak Senudu

Viswak is a 16-year-old college student who writes about love, heartbreak, and motivation. He blends his poems with real life experiences that connect with his readers, and with a love for language and literature, Viswak hopes to embark on a career as a poet.

## Mx. Adam Khan

Adam is a non-binary, neurodivergent social activist who, alongside studies, has been empowering marginalised communities across the West Midlands. Adam has been exploring different methods marginalised communities express feelings, experiences, and stories.

## Natalie Carr

Natalie Carr is a British poet and author living in Redditch in the midlands. She is a self-employed mother of two who uses her experiences of motherhood and suffering with mental health problems to write and connect with others. Her aim with her writing is to make sure no one ever feels alone in their struggles, and to encourage more people to use writing to help them on their journey to healing.

## Niamh Baxter

Niamh is currently a student studying illustration at the University of Worcester. Alongside her studies, she joined the Poetry Society – and led it to success as the 2022-23 chair – while developing a love for reading, writing, and sharing poetry! She enjoys writing poetry to express feelings and deal with emotions, whilst allowing her to be creative without limitations. Plus, she loves using repetition in 80% of her work.

## Oly Bliss

Oly works at the Hive Library and is a freelance artist. He has been living in Worcester since 2019 with his partner Craig and their two cats Arti and Otto. He enjoys Sugar Daddy's Iced Coffees, Little Bento Box Sushi and can be spotted searching for fairy Pokémon with Craig. He is also a member of seam collective, an artist led group of textile artists.

## Quinn Cross

Quinn is an acting, theatre and performance student who enjoys writing poetry to explore different themes, articulate her feelings about difficult topics, and to express love and hope. She is trying to push for a better future for everyone through her poetry.

## Rachy xox

Rach is on a journey from trauma to healing, at 40 years old is new to poetry but loves nothing more than feeling inspired and sharing it, in the hope that it may help someone on their journey too.

## Rhi Armstrong

Rhi is a vibrant, young poet new to the Worcester poetry scene. She helps run the University of Worcester Poetry Society while obtaining her degree in English Literature and Creative Writing. She is an avid writer on topics such as mental health, relationships, and pure feminist rage.

## Rhianna Levi

Rhianna is a writer, teacher and academic based in Worcester, England. She is a former Worcestershire Poet Laureate and is the 2023 Worcester Carnival Queen. Alongside the publication of her debut poetry collection, Mortal Veins (2023), Rhianna has been published in numerous anthologies and literature mags. Rhianna has degrees from both the University of Worcester and Birmingham City University. As a writer and holistic educator, her work empathises the complexity of humanity and existentialism that in itself is a remarkable phenomenon.

## Robin Cain

Robin is a fourth-year student studying a masters in Touring Theatre. Their passion for poetry began in 2022 during a Writing for Performance lecture. Along with competing at the national university poetry competition, UniSlam, and getting Worcester to the semi-finals, they are performing at the 2023 Edinburgh Fringe with their theatre company MissingLink Theatre. Burnt Lavender is a show that explores conversion therapy using spoken word, physical theatre, and jarring designs.

## Ruth Stacey

Ruth Stacey is a poet from Worcestershire. Her books include Queen, Jewel, Mistress (2015), Inheritance (2017), I, Ursula (2020), The Dark Room: Letters to Krista (2021). Her forthcoming book is about the tarot artist Pamela Colman Smith.

## Sage White-Drake

Sage is a local Agender Enby. They practise creative writing through short stories, Dungeons & Dragons campaigns, and occasionally some comedy. Despite zero technical training, Sage has always wanted to try poetry. Their self-confessed style is 'word salad gone wrong'. However, if even one person smiles or laughs, then it's all been towards a good goal.

## Susan Wood

Poetry has been of great importance to Susan for most of her life, finding inspiration in nature, reflection, and whatever catches her imagination. An active member of The Lichfield Poets, she has had work published in a variety of charity anthologies, and contributes to many Open Mic and community events. These include PoArtry, Poetry for Ukraine, and Fuse Festival. She also paints and illustrates, and has worked with writers to illustrate their books for publication. She won the inaugural Mal Dewhirst Creative Writing Award 2022.

## Tommy Bjørheim

Tommy is a Norwegian student at University of Worcester, who has been using poetry to express creativity and difficult thoughts. The poetry he writes is often about unfairness in the world, bad relationships, and taboo topics like self-harm and suicide.

## Zoe Dempsey Martínez

Zoe is a twenty-year-old Creative Writing and Illustration student from the North of Spain. Their multimedia work often explores childhood, nature, and identity, as well as delving into protest art as a queer neurodiverse poet. They are passionate about celebrating all art as an accessible form of therapy, activism, and community healing.

# COLOUR THEORY

Worcester's Student
Poetry Society and friends